Environment: A World of Change

Dona Herweck Rice

Consultants

Sally Creel, Ed.D.
Curriculum Consultant

Leann Iacuone, M.A.T., NBCT, ATC
Riverside Unified School District

Image Credits: p.16 (top) Steve Bloom Images/Alamy; p.10 (top) Stocktrek Images, Inc./Alamy; pp.10–11 (background), 11 (top), iStock; p.22 Andrew Rakoczy/Science Source; p.20 Dan Guravich/Science Source; p.3 Scott Linstead/Science Source; p.24 Tom McHugh/Science Source; pp.28–29 (illustrations) Janelle Bell-Martin; all other images from Shutterstock.

Teacher Created Materials
5301 Oceanus Drive
Huntington Beach, CA 92649-1030
http://www.tcmpub.com

ISBN 978-1-4807-4602-2

Printed by: VIN#973
Printed In: China
PO11140

Table of Contents

Counting on Change

Some people say that the only thing that stays the same is change.

In this world, change is something we can count on. What is here today may be gone tomorrow. Or if it is not gone, it may not be the same. Day becomes night. Seeds become plants. Food becomes waste. And you grow up and become an adult!

Yes, you can count on it. Change is here to stay!

Night turns into day.

Kids grow up and become adults.

Seeds grow into plants.

World of Nature

Let's start with the big world around us. Our land, water, and air seem pretty set as they are. It is hard to imagine them changing. But they do.

Water changes the land.

Water Cycle

The water in the water cycle is everywhere—on, below, and above Earth.

Water

Water is part of a cycle that is constantly changing. Water in its liquid form heats up and becomes a gas. The gas rises into the air. It cools and comes back to Earth as rain and snow. Or it freezes and becomes ice. **Temperature** changes water's form. It changes and changes some more. Who knows? The water you swim in today may partly be made of the water you bathed in last year!

Rocks

Rocks seem pretty solid, don't they? It's hard to imagine them changing. But they do, of course. They break down, and they come together.

Rocks can be broken down, bit by bit. It happens through **weathering**. That is the process by which wind and water break away at rocks. They become **sediment**. These are rock bits and pieces, such as gravel, sand, and dust. When wind or water moves the sediment, it is called **erosion**.

Heat and pressure also can change rocks. Some rocks melt into magma when heated. Some change from one type of rock into another. Sediments also can be pressed into new rocks.

magma

Rock Types

There are three types of rock: *igneous*, *metamorphic*, and *sedimentary*. Rocks can change from one type to another through the rock cycle. The rock cycle is shown in the chart below.

Volcanoes and Earthquakes

Earth is always moving. But the land itself moves, too. The top layer of land is made of **plates**. The plates bump and glide against each other. We do not usually feel or see most of this movement. But sometimes we do—in a big way! Earthquakes may rumble, and volcanoes may erupt as the plates move. When this happens, the land itself changes form.

Mt. Stromboli, off the coast of Italy, has been erupting for 2,000 years!

Fires and Floods

Fires and floods are a normal part of nature. Nature clears away old and dead plant life through fires. Floods happen all the time, too. They may move large amounts of dirt and rip up trees and plants. They change the shape of the land.

World of Living Things

Every living thing on Earth changes, too. Things change every day. That is the circle of life.

Growing Up

Seeds grow. Puppies grow. Babies grow. Living things start young and new. They grow and grow each day until they reach **maturity**. Maturity is when they are fully grown. For people, we call this *adulthood*.

Even when living things have grown to their full size, they still keep changing. They are made of cells. Cells die, and new cells grow all the time. Plants grow new leaves and buds. People grow new skin and hair and make new blood. As long as they live, living things grow and change.

The oil palm takes three to four years to reach maturity.

Dying

Of course, living things do not live forever. Some live for a short time, such as a mayfly that lives for just one day. Some live for thousands of years, such as quaking aspen trees. But disease, accident, or old age finally ends every life, and the growing stops.

When a living thing dies, its body **decomposes**. It breaks down and turns into **nutrients** for the soil. This **nourishes** new plants and helps life on Earth continue.

Seagrass

Scientists have discovered seagrass that is more than 100,000 years old!

Every living thing dies.

New Life

But death is not the end of the story. New life begins all the time. Plants die, but seeds grow in their place. Animals die, but young animals take their place. People die, but babies are born every day.

These bear cubs will grow up one day.

The cycle of life, death, and new life is called the *circle of life.* It keeps going around and around. As long as living things have the water, food, and space they need to live, life continues.

Of course, if they don't have what they need, that is another story.

A mother flamingo takes care of her baby chick.

Seals must live near water.

Going, Going, Gone!

A living thing is called an *organism*. Every living thing is part of a habitat. This is the area in which it lives. It has what it needs to live well. An organism lives in its habitat because it is just right for a good and healthy

Penguins need a cold habitat.

life. The right food, water, weather, and shelter are there. The air and water are clean. The organism needs these **conditions** to stay the same. Its body is made for them.

Sometimes, the conditions in nature change. The weather may get warmer or colder over time. The land may change through plate movement, fire, floods, or more. Water sources may dry up. Food sources may go away.

Polar bears have **adapted** to live in very cold places. They have two layers of fur and four inches of fat to keep them warm.

The organisms in a habitat must adapt. They must change to deal with the new conditions. Or they must move to a new place. If they do not do one of these things, they will probably die out.

Camels have adapted to live in very dry places. Their humps are full of fat that they can use when food and water are scarce.

Sometimes, it is not nature but people that change a habitat. We pollute the land, water, and air. We tear down habitats to build roads, homes, and businesses. We introduce organisms that do not belong in that habitat, and they change the balance of nature there. They harm the living things. Non-native plants may crowd out native plants and become extra fire dangers as well.

Coyote Trouble

In some places, coyotes are a problem for people. They may attack and eat pets. But people have invaded the coyotes' habitats and have taken away their food sources. The coyotes are adapting to the new conditions.

As our population grows, we crowd into animal and plant habitats. We take over their homes, and they may have nowhere else to go.

People cut down this forest. It may have been home to many animals.

Whether by nature or people, some animals and plants are in danger of not surviving. They become **endangered**. If they are not able to survive, they become extinct. This means they are gone forever.

Dragons

A small lizard called a *draco volans* has large folds of skin. These folds let it glide up to 30 feet. It looks like a dragon—but it does not breathe fire!

Many types of plants and animals that used to live on Earth are now extinct. The most famous of these may be dinosaurs. Dinosaurs once ruled the world. Now, their bones are the only reminders we have of life from long, long ago.

Scientists say that birds may be related to dinosaurs.

Today and Every Day

So, life and planet Earth move on. There is birth and growth, death and new life. There is fire and flood and movement, and the landscape changes.

Change is part of life and part of Earth. When we wake up each day, we know that on this day and every day forward, there will be change.

In fact, we can count on it!

How do you think this erupting volcano will change the land around it?

Let's Do Science!

How do living things change? See for yourself!

What to Get

- fast-growing seeds, such as lima beans
- paper and pencil
- pot with potting soil
- water

What to Do

1. Plant a few seeds in the soil, and add water.

2. Put the pot in a sunny place.

3. Observe the pot each day at the same time, and add some water as needed. Draw what you see.

4. Keep observing and drawing daily. What changes do you notice?

Glossary

adapted—changed to deal with new conditions

conditions—circumstances; the way that things are

decomposes—causes something to be slowly broken down after death

endangered—in danger of dying out

erosion—movement of weathered rock and sediment

maturity—the age of full development; adulthood

nourishes—provides with food for life and growth

nutrients—substances that living things need to live and grow

plates—large sections of land in the top layer of Earth's surface

sediment—very small pieces of rock, such as sand, gravel, and dust

temperature—the measurement of heat in something

weathering—the slow breakdown of rock and sediment

Index

Your Turn!

Decomposing Fruit

What happens when something decomposes? Watch for yourself. Find an old piece of fruit. Look at it every day. Write a paragraph about what you see. Use a lot of adjectives and adverbs!